Extraordinary
moments with God

Extraordinary Moments with God

by Michelle Spencer

Published by Michelle Spencer

Chancery Lane, Christ Church

Facebook Michelle Spencer

Instagram @michellep7111

Copyright © 2023 Michelle Spencer

All rights reserved. No portion of this book may be reproduced in any form without permission from the publisher, except as permitted by Barbados copyright law.

For permissions contact:

michellep7111@gmail.com

Cover by Michelle Spencer

ABOUT THE AUTHOR

Michelle Spencer is a woman who loves the Lord and lots of laughter. When it comes to her walk with her Father though, she considers it to be serious business.

Michelle resides on the beautiful island of Barbados and is the mother of two young men. She is a broadcaster with more than twenty years experience and she thoroughly enjoys doing her morning show where she is affectionately known as Principal Michelle, having created the fictional school called Life University over the airwaves through the imagination and creativity given by the Holy Spirit.

Michelle hopes that the words of this book and the meditation that will be in your heart will be pleasing to God and create change in your life.

TABLE OF CONTENTS

1. Guidance in the darkness 7
2. Focus on the finish 11
3. Toeing the line 15
4. First things first 19
5. Senseless shadows 23
6. Look up! 27
7. Heat helps 31
8. Welcome home 35
9. Brand new 39
10. Imperfect perspective 43
11. GPS 46
12. Answer the call 50
13. You stink! 54
14. In hot pursuit 58
15. Release the flow 62
16. Bear with me 65
17. Standout blooms 69
18. A tender touch 72
19. No pain, no gain 75
20. Be careful little eyes 78
21. Out of sorts 81

FOREWORD

*Then He said, "Go out, and stand on the mountain before the Lord." And behold, the Lord passed by, and a great and strong wind tore into the mountains and broke the rocks in pieces before the Lord, but the Lord was not in the wind; and after the wind an earthquake, but the Lord was not in the earthquake; and after the earthquake a fire, but the Lord was not in the fire; and after the fire **a still small voice**.*
1 Kings 19:11-12

    Have you ever wanted God to speak to you clearly so that there is no doubt that He is getting your attention and sending you a message?

    Trust me, God speaks just like that and in ways that we often miss. Why do we miss it? Because we don't expect to find a great, big, wonderful God in the midst of the common. But that is exactly where He is. He started in the lowliest of places in a manger, in a small town. He spoke to the lowliest of persons first - the shepherds - even before word of his appearance reached a king's ears.

So God is not a stranger to the ordinary.

I want to encourage you, through the following experiences, to look constantly for God and to listen to his voice. He is there and He is speaking. As you go through this book may you prayerfully read and open your heart to what He is whispering. Write those thoughts and meditate on the Word. May God share himself with you and make ordinary moments **extraordinary**.

1. Guidance in the darkness

Psalm 32:8
I will instruct you and teach you in the way you should go; I will counsel you with my eye upon you.

We are creatures of habit. You have a routine as to how you get ready: you bathe at a certain time, brush your teeth a certain way, comb or brush your hair just so. We follow certain paths or roads to work. Habit. Yes.

What happens if God interrupts your sequence of events? Are you upset and offset? Is your attitude one of 'not today Lord' or do you willingly follow where he leads.

Recently mine was tossed aside just like that. Early one morning before the sun even rose I was on my way to work. I normally take one of two ways and just as I was leaving home I heard very clearly… 'You need to follow where I am leading today'.

I was like what? I got in the car and started my journey. Then I heard… 'Turn here'. Okkk. Then at another junction I heard, 'Turn there'.

This was not my usual travel route, but I heard the voice often enough that when I was approaching a turn or intersection I slowed to listen as to the next way to go. Some of the instructions were last minute, but I made the turns. I eventually came to a familiar road and there, at that hour of the morning, was a friend walking on the road. I nearly didn't recognise her in the darkness, but I pulled over and offered her a ride.

When I reached my destination I marvelled at how God had led me to her. We both concluded that maybe, just maybe, there were reasons beyond our knowledge for my twists and turns that morning.

Perhaps God was protecting her from danger and I was just the vehicle, so to speak, for her safety. Maybe He was protecting me and got me off the normal path. We might never know but, what I do know, is what he said to me afterwards.

He said, "You will need to follow me just like you did this morning. You might not know where you are going or why and some of the turns will be quick and last minute, but if you listen, I will lead."

Dear friend, are you listening to the instructions God is giving you today? Do they seem strange and unfamiliar? Are you slowing down to listen? Trust that he knows what He's doing and the why, and follow every turn on this marvellous journey with the one who **is** the Way.

Prayer:
Lord may my ears be open to hear what you say and my heart be willing to go where you lead, in Jesus name, amen.

Your thoughts:

2. Focus on the finish

Proverbs 4:25
Let your eyes look straight ahead; fix your gaze directly before you.

It was night time and I was taking a friend home. The rain began to drizzle softly. We travelled in silence for a while then suddenly a question broke the stillness.

"Doesn't that bother you?" my friend asked.

"What?" I replied.

"Seeing those drops on the windscreen," she said. "I was here waiting for you to turn on the wipers."

I said, "Honestly I didn't even see them. I am looking at the road, not the windscreen."

Then the familiar voice of the Lord whispered, "Now there is a lesson." Immediately I got it. Oftentimes we are so distracted by what's immediately ahead of us that we can't fix our gaze on where we are going. Sometimes we are silently becoming annoyed as well that others aren't seeing what we are seeing and doing something about it.

As the passenger, my friend was somewhat helpless in that situation. I, like God, was looking at the end and the way to get there. I knew that lives were in my hands and had to navigate the darkness to reach our journey's end safely. We might be asking, 'God can't you see what's right there?' We might also be wondering if He's not going to remove it.

My challenge to you is that you "let your eyes look straight ahead" as it says in Proverbs. The raindrops on the windscreen aren't your focus. Don't be shortsighted, but look past them to where you are going and concentrate on the destination. Trust that God sees and knows what He's doing as we travel along in the dark, rainy times.

Prayer:
Heavenly Father, forgive me for the times that I've become flustered over the things and situations that are immediately in view. Help me to look ahead to where you are carefully taking me. In Jesus name I pray, amen.

Your thoughts:
_____
_____
_____
_____
_____
_____
_____
_____
_____
_____
_____

3. *Toeing the line*

Proverbs 3:6
In all thy ways acknowledge him, and he shall direct thy paths.

Have you ever thought to let God dress you? I mean on a daily basis let him pick out your clothes. I never did until I started taking that verse for today seriously. When it says in all your ways acknowledge him, it means just that… ALL.

One day I was getting ready for work and God told me what to wear, down to the very shoes. The outfit was nice, but I didn't care too much for the shoes. I preferred another pair, sandals to be precise. These ones that God picked out were enclosed shoes and I really didn't feel like having my feet cooped up all day. I didn't even really like the shoes and wondered why I even bought them. Nevertheless God insisted. I reluctantly obeyed.

When I was exiting work for the day I pulled a heavy door to leave and would you believe I opened that door on my toes! It barely hurt because my feet were protected by God's selection of shoes that day. Well you know I just stood there and marvelled. Had it not been for God telling me what to wear I would have injured my foot. What a great protector! God cares even about our toes.

Let's go back to our verse… To acknowledge means to recognize the rights, authority or status of. Have you started to let God have his rightful place in your life? Do you let him exercise his authority over what you do? Is he supreme in your decision making? If you haven't started, now is a good time to begin. I'm sure he will guide you daily and protect you as well, all the way down to your toes.

Prayer:

Lord forgive me for running my life my way and ignoring you and what you want for me. Help me to come to you with all things in Jesus name, amen.

Your thoughts:

_____
_____
_____
_____
_____
_____
_____
_____
_____
_____
_____

4. First things first

Matthew 6:33

"But seek first the kingdom of God and his righteousness, and all these things will be added to you."

It was minutes after four in the morning and I was washing dishes and putting away wares. Like who does that at that hour? But there I was at that time attending to household chores.

I had a set of glasses of varying sizes to stow away, along with some jugs. I put the glasses in the cupboard and then tried my best to put away the jugs. For the life of me it just was not working. With every try something was still left on the countertop. This was becoming frustrating. I literally stood and stared at the space trying to remember how it was stacked before and I just couldn't.

Then as clear as day I heard: "Put in the big things first." Okkkkk. So I started with the biggest jug all the way down to the smallest glass. They all miraculously fit. Again I just stood and stared.

How did that happen? What was the secret?

Then I heard again: "Now do that with your life."

I shook my head in disbelief. I know that it is often a struggle to get everything done, but I never considered that I was neglecting to properly prioritise what should fit into my life or how. I thought I was doing well by putting everything on my calendar and checking it before I agreed to any other commitments. But somehow something always seemed to be left out.

How about you? Are you putting in the big things first? What's big on your list? God. Family. Friends. Work. How about exercise or self care or even rest? Ask God to show you what are the real priorities and how to order them. Find

out the difference between the important and the urgent and sort your life to suit. God wants first place and it's up to us to give it, rather than Him taking it.
May we seek Him and his kingdom before anything else.

Prayer:
Heavenly Father you have been patiently sitting on the sidelines waiting to be put in your rightful place. Help me God to always seek you first in any and everything in Jesus name, amen.

Your thoughts:
_____
_____
_____
_____
_____
_____
_____
_____

5. Senseless shadows

John 8:31-32
So Jesus said to the Jews who had believed him, "If you abide in my word, you are truly my disciples, and you will know the truth, and the truth will set you free."

    We are creatures of habit and I am no exception to that rule. So every day I take one of a couple of roads to work. On that early morning drive in the darkness there is a particular tree at the side of the street that casts a shadow in the shape of a man standing in the middle of the road.
    When I first started travelling that route, nine times out of ten I would think there was someone standing there and I would end up braking to avoid a collision.
    One morning, true to form, I saw the man-shaped shadow from afar off and I was about to brake when I heard

God whisper, "Are you going to trust what you see or what you know?"
That thought hit hard in my spirit.
Too often we are fooled by what we see and the things we know go through the window. That morning I had to acknowledge that I rely on what's in front of me too often as opposed to what I know to be true.

Jesus is the way, the truth and the life and the Holy Spirit promises to guide us into all truth. It also says in John 8:32 that you will *know* the truth and the truth will set you free.

Well let me tell you, that morning I was set free from the anxiety of causing an accident and running over an imaginary person. I knew that what I was seeing was just a shadow and there was nothing in my path.

Are you looking more at your imagined reality rather than God's truth? What God says is far more real than the silhouettes from satan that he casts in front of us to distract and disturb our journey.

    Trust what you know.

Prayer:
Father, I ask you to help me to focus on you and your word to guide me. I ask that I will not be distracted by the shadows that the enemy throws in front of me, but I will remember that your Word is truth and trust what I know of you. In Jesus name, amen.

Your thoughts:

_____

_____

_____

_____

_____

_____

_____

_____

6. Look up!

Psalm 84:2
I long, yes, I faint with longing to enter the courts of the Lord.
With my whole being, body and soul, I will shout joyfully to the living God.

    A friend wanted to do some landscaping on her property. She just wanted greenery. No flowers, just greenery. And it had to be palms, but not just any palm, it had to have a certain look. From that moment she decided she wanted those trees, she started seeing them everywhere.
    "I've travelled this road so often and it is only now that I realise palms are here," she said.
    "Yup, that happens," I said. "It's like when you decide to buy a car, you begin to pay more attention to cars. And if you want a certain one. You start seeing it everywhere."

"Yeeeahhh," she agreed.

And as she nodded I heard God ask me, "So what are you looking at and longing for? Is it me so you see me everywhere or is your focus elsewhere?"

I really had to ponder. Then I whispered a little prayer in my heart asking God to help me to see him first with my heart and then with my eyes.

The psalmist said his soul faints with longing for the Lord. Is my desire for God that deep? Is yours? Have you set your heart on seeking him so much that you look for him everywhere?
It says in Colossians 3: "If ye then be risen with Christ seek those things which are above." That same chapter encourages us to set our affection on those things as well. May God help us to focus heavenward.

Prayer:

Dear God, we know the things we see on this earth seem far more real than those things that are above, but help me God to look on the things that are eternal and to see you every day, everywhere. In Jesus name, amen.

Your thoughts:

_____

_____

_____

_____

_____

_____

_____

_____

_____

_____

_____

_____

_____

_____

_____

_____

7. Heat helps
James 1:2
My brethren count it all joy when you fall into various trials, knowing that the testing of your faith produces patience.

Are you a tea baby or a coffee child? Do you have your special mug that you have to use? I'm not one who likes hot beverages, but I was given a mug by my nephew. He and my son got together and surprised me with one that has my picture on it.

The reason it is all the more special is the fact that they found a picture I actually like and they put some kind words of affection on the mug that speak to my character.

This mug though, under normal circumstances is completely black and ordinary. Nothing to draw your attention to it. But guess what? When hot water goes into that cup, it comes alive. That picture glows and those words about me can be read by anyone.

God recently made me see this mug differently. You see, it was a tough season and I was having a cup of hot chocolate one day when I heard him whisper, "I am bringing out your character in the midst of this heat just like this mug." If I were to personify the mug I am sure that it didn't like hot water one bit, but it was made for it. The beauty of the design came out with the heat.

That was my lesson that day. I was designed for the heat and others would see all that the maker had designed me to be because of it.

So dear friend, are you in the fire right now? Take heart. God is trying to bring the beauty out of you too. I know it is easier said than done, but yes count it all joy and in verse four of James 1 says, "...let patience have her perfect work, that you may be perfect and complete, lacking nothing."

Remember as well that the hot water cools at some point. So your trial is just for a season.

Prayer:
Heavenly Father, trials are not easy but help me to stay in the heat and persevere so that you can perfect me. In Jesus name, amen.

Your thoughts:

_____
_____
_____
_____
_____
_____
_____
_____
_____
_____

8. Welcome home

Luke 15:20
And he arose and came to his father. But while he was still a long way off, his father saw him and felt compassion, and ran and embraced him and kissed him.

Have you ever had a loved one that you knew was going down the wrong path and you could do nothing to help?

You can clearly see him/her on the downward spiral, on the slippery slope and you know that no amount of talking, pleading or even shouting can bring that person back.

I've had that experience. I watched someone near and dear to me completely ignore all the warning signs and go head long into oncoming traffic. Not in a literal sense, but it felt that way.

One day we were in the same house and he was in another room singing along to some of his favourite songs. I thought about how much I loved him and I wished I could make his life better. At that moment, God whispered, "Imagine how much *I* love him."

I had to pause because as much as I tried I knew I could never love as much as God did. And as much as I hurt because of the situation, I was pretty sure God was hurting even more.

Are you facing a situation where you are hurting on behalf of a loved one. Well let's remember that God specialises in bringing loved ones back to himself. HIs love compels them to come home and his love causes him to go after lost sheep.

Place that loved one in God's hands and leave him there. Trust the one who looks at us from afar off with love and runs to meet us with hugs and kisses. He can bring the prodigal home.

Prayer:

Almighty God, it's not easy seeing my family and friends go astray but you are more than able to bring them back. Watch over them Lord and guide them safely back to your fold. In Jesus name amen.

Your thoughts:

_____
_____
_____
_____
_____
_____
_____
_____
_____
_____
_____

9. Brand new

Revelation 21:5
He who was seated on the throne said, "I am making everything new!" Then he said, "Write this down, for these words are trustworthy and true."

Have you ever had a makeover? Or thought you need one? How about a room in your home? Have you ever refreshed that?

At the beginning of the year, the month or even a week there is a brand new opportunity to start afresh and we wait for that time to come to start putting things in place.

Recently I decided to change my name. It was a decision that I was toying around with for a bit but then the opportunity came and I just did it. Little did I know how much of a change it would be and it turned out to be quite a process. The identification card had to be changed, my driver's licence, and documents at various institutions. It was a lot and it couldn't all be done in one day. At some point along this journey I heard God whisper, as he normally does, "This is just how I am making you over. I am changing you and your identity in the same way. I am making you new. Little by little."

I breathed deeply because if there is one question that many of us struggle with it is "Who am I?" So to hear God say I was being made over made me wonder who I would become.

Perhaps you have had a life changing situation as well that altered your way of thinking and your attitude. You now see things and perhaps people differently. I pray that this is a positive change, like mine was. You might not have a whole new identity like I do, but I am believing that your transformation is for your good.

As it says in our verse today, may you hear God telling you he's making things new. May things you have longed for and prayed about that seem old and stale be changed. And if He has given you that word, then write it down because it is trustworthy and true and wait for it to come to pass.

Prayer:
God sometimes we are stuck in the past and in the old. May we experience times of refreshing with you. You are the God who gives new mercies on a daily basis so I pray we will see the changes you have promised in our lives as we patiently wait. In Jesus name, amen.

Your thoughts:

_____

_____

_____

_____

_____

_____

10. Imperfect perspective

Ecclesiastes 3:11
He has made everything beautiful in its time.

    I was sitting with someone the other day and just as she reached for her glasses the frame broke. After expressing surprise at the ease with which it happened, she reached for some clear tape to do a temporary fix until she could get them repaired. With a bit of "MacGyvering" they were put back together and then there was a concern. When she put them on all she could see was the tape. I told her I couldn't see it. That tape sat perfected camouflaged on her lens. *She* was the only one who could see it.

    At that moment God said, "That is exactly how you operate." Sometimes all we can see is our brokenness and our flaws. It is our only focus. Noone else

notices, but because it is right in our face that's all we can see.
We may even end up being embarrassed because we think others notice our insufficiency, or the fact that we seem to be barely holding together. We think of ourselves of ugly and messed up. But God is also saying bring the pieces to him. Let him make us whole. Let him make us beautiful.

Prayer:
Lord, I bring all my imperfections and my brokenness to you. I ask that you make me whole again. Help me to look past them and to focus on who I am in you and where you are taking me as I trust in you. In Jesus name, amen.

Your thoughts:

_____

_____

_____

_____

11. GPS

Psalm 32:8
I will instruct you and teach you in the way you should go; I will guide you with My eye.

There hardly seems to be a time when there is no traffic and with my business I always need to have the fastest and easiest route to where I am going. No wonder I employ a GPS system most of the time. This particular day was no different. I had a delivery to make in a familiar area, but so that I wouldn't get lost on the way I decided to put the address into Google maps.
I was taken off the beaten path.
At first I thought, "Oh gosh! This thing is malfunctioning." But despite the thought I decided to follow the directions.
Eventually I came to a familiar area which was parallel to the road I

would normally take. When I looked to my left there was a whole line of bumper to bumper traffic that I know would have taken quite a while to get through. I said "Thank God I followed". And God said, "You're thanking me for getting you through traffic? How about letting me get you through life."

He clearly stated that just like that little man-made device could help me to navigate and pick the best route to my destination, He was more than able to do the same for me.

Our God knows what is up ahead and how to avoid traffic and divert us to the paths we should take. As a matter of fact He says I am the way. He tells us in today's verse that He will guide us. Why not trust him today to help you to avoid delays as well. He is more than able.

Prayer:
Father forgive us for trusting in things man has made that are prone to fail

more than we trust you. Help us to put our total confidence in you and may you direct our paths. In Jesus name, amen.

Your thoughts:

12. Answer the call

Revelation 3:30
Behold I stand at the door and knock. If any man hear my voice, and open the door, I will come in to him and will sup with him, and he with me.

    Have you ever missed or ignored a call for whatever reason? Well that has happened to me on more than one occasion. Maybe the phone was on silent or I was busy but for whatever reason I didn't answer the phone. Recently I missed a call from my sister and when I called back she was not available.
    As a matter of fact she had left home altogether to go to an outing that I was pretty sure she would've allowed me to tag along.
    I sat there a bit annoyed with myself for missing the call. At that moment, I heard the gentlest voice whisper, "You miss opportunities from

me in the same way. Sometimes you know you are to meet with me or to answer when I call and you miss it."

I said, "Wow Lord." And I sat there wondering how many times there was something he wanted to tell me or show me or even somewhere he wanted to take me and the chance just passed me by.

Friend, so often we call out to God and we expect him to answer, and not just answer, but to come running. However, we don't return the favour. Like it says in the verse, he isn't only knocking, but He is calling to us as well. I hope that we will pay attention when He's at the door trying to gain access to our lives.

Prayer:
Lord forgive me for ignoring when you call or for being unavailable to even hear and answer. Help me to make time for you and to listen out for the

opportunities to spend time in fellowship with you. In Jesus name, amen.

Your thoughts:

_____
_____
_____
_____
_____
_____
_____
_____
_____
_____
_____
_____
_____
_____

13. You stink!

Romans 3:23
For all have sinned and come short of the glory of God.

I do quite a bit of driving and at odd hours sometimes so it's been my habit, for safety reasons, to drive with the windows up. I am in my own little world, enjoying my music or quiet time. I seem to do my best thinking on the road.

However, recently I decided to get some fresh air and I rolled the windows down while on one of my journeys. That did not last five minutes. Soon I was back in the comfort of my AC enclosure and the reason: the world smelled. There was exhaust, a garbage truck, all sorts of smells. I couldn't take it. So I said to myself, "Well no wonder I keep the windows up." No sooner did I say that than God replied, "You know you are no better right."

I was puzzled. What could God mean? I guess He heard me questioning in my heart and He said, "You are no better than the world you are trying to get away from. I died for your sins the same way I died for theirs and all the sins smell."

Talk about conviction.

Since then I have had a new perspective every time I roll the windows down to get some air.

Are you thinking you are better than those around you because you are saved and sanctified? Be reminded like the verse says, we have all sinned and fallen short of God's glory.

Prayer:
God may we never look down on the people around us. We all need you to clean us up and make us new. You said anyone who comes to you will be a brand new creature. Help us God to

introduce others to you so that we can all be clothed in your glory. In Jesus name, amen.

Your thoughts:

14. In hot pursuit

Psalm 23:6
Surely your goodness and love will follow me all the days of my life, and I will dwell in the house of the Lord forever.

We're always hearing warnings about travelling alone at night. Lock your doors. Have the windows up. Don't stop for anything or anyone.
I've always heeded this advice since it seemed to be the right thing to do.
Recently these warnings all came flooding back when I was driving at around 430am. I glanced in the rear view mirror and there was a vehicle with lots of headlamps in a distance quickly approaching. The driver really seemed to be in a hurry and soon enough, he caught up with me and was tailing me. I thought this was strange, but decided

not to panic. After all I thought if they wanted to do me harm they wouldn't have so many headlamps on to draw attention to themselves. So I continued on my journey, but still decided to be cautious.

It was then that I heard God whisper, "That is how goodness and mercy will follow you." Well I nearly let out a praise shout right then and there because there was this vehicle right at the back of me. First it was a distance away and eventually, because of the speed at which it was travelling it caught up to me. It was as if there was purpose in this person's driving. Then it had so many lights that when it came up close those lights illuminated my path so much that I wondered if my own headlights were still on.

That's just how God comes after us; with purpose. I thank God for His grace, HIs goodness, His love and His mercy that continue to pursue us. May you see the continued goodness of God in your darkness as well.

Prayer:
God, your lovingkindness is better than life. We thank you for always showing us your grace and mercy. May we never take them for granted. In Jesus name, amen.

Your thoughts:

_____
_____
_____
_____
_____
_____
_____
_____
_____

15. Release the flow

Psalm 42:1
As the deer pants for the stream of water, so my soul pants for you, my God.

If I never believed in global warming and climate change I do now. Temperatures are absolutely soaring this summer. As a result it is water, water and more water. There are more showers taken and more drinking of this precious liquid.

I own a huge water bottle. It's a gallon bottle that anyone who sees it marvels at the size. One day I was refilling my "tank" from the jug in the fridge and looking forward to a long, refreshing drink. Then came a quiet whisper, "Take the cover off and it will fill quicker."

Now this wasn't a new action. I had done that several times before.

What was different about this time is what God said afterwards. He said, "You need to uncap me just like the water jug. I want to fill you quickly, but you are stopping the flow."

I obediently took the cover off and I was transfixed looking at that water flow into the bottle with far greater ease and so much more speed. Then and there I purposed in my heart to open up and let God in.

What about you? Are you stopping what God wants to do in your life and only accepting a trickle of his love, or his might? Why not release the flow of God into your life as well.

Prayer:
God I repent. I am sorry that I have only given you limited access to me. But God I want the living water in abundance and may it flow out of me like a mighty gushing stream as a source of refreshment to those around me. In Jesus name, amen.

Your thoughts:

16. Bear with me

Ephesians 4:1 & 2
I therefore, a prisoner for the Lord, urge you to walk in a manner worthy of the calling to which you have been called, with all humility and gentleness, with patience, bearing with one another in love.

Have you ever heard the phrase "walk a mile in my shoes"? I am pretty sure you have.

This phrase tries to sensitise us to the need to place ourselves in someone else's situation before we pass judgement. And we know it is really easy to judge, especially when we don't have all the facts.

Recently God gently tapped me on the shoulder and reminded me of my tendency to judge too.

You see my right indicator light to the front of my vehicle stopped working so any driver coming in the opposite direction would not notice that I wanted to turn and would probably tell me off. My light was not immediately fixed because I didn't have the funds to get the job done. Amazingly I started to notice other vehicles with similar issues. Some didn't have the rear brake lights working, while others may not have had the light at all.

And just like that I started to empathise with the owners. Perhaps they didn't have the money right now either to do those repairs. And true to form God whispered in my ear, "See how much more tolerant you are since you are in the same position? How about trying tolerance with other things." I sighed a big sigh and recognised that once again God was right.

What about you? Are you only sympathetic and empathetic when you have been in a similar circumstance? How about lovingly bearing with that brother or sister because it is only by the grace of God that you are not the one in that position.

Prayer:
Father, I thank you for alerting me to the needs and circumstances of others. Help me to be more like you in looking out for and meeting those needs and to be more compassionate, loving and kind. In Jesus name, amen.

Your thoughts:

_____
_____
_____
_____
_____
_____
_____
_____
_____

17. Standout blooms

Matthew 5:16
Let your light so shine before men, that they may see your good works, and glorify your Father which is in heaven.

We were in the middle of a drought and all around was dry and brown. Cracked earth was everywhere and there was just a dreary feeling on the land. I was driving along, minding my own business, when suddenly my attention was drawn to some bright yellow flowers along the roadside.

How was it even possible that in the midst of the brown they were blooming and looked so cheery?

God whispered, "You need to be like that."

"Like what?" I replied.

He said, "In the midst of all the dryness in the world you need to stand out like those flowers."

I got the message. This world is full of hardship, sorrow and pain.

Enough to drain the life and liveliness out of anyone. I needed to let the world see God's hope and life, just like the brilliant hues of those flowers drew my eyes to them. You just couldn't help but notice them. They were like beacons!

I know each of us has our own struggles but if you can help to brighten someone's path why not do so? Someone just might return the favour.

Prayer:
Father, help us to be a light in this darkened world and a haven of hope when there is none. May we stand out in the midst of confusion and chaos and be a source of hope pointing others to you. In Jesus name, amen.

Your thoughts:

18. A tender touch

Psalm 34:18
The LORD is close to the brokenhearted and saves those who are crushed in spirit.

Do you have anything of value that you use on a regular basis? How do you treat it? How would you feel if it were to become damaged?

This was my plight when my headphones became damaged. I don't even know how they got broken but they did. I sighed. What now Lord? Do I throw them away? Buy a new pair? What should I do?

I examined them and realised that they still worked and perhaps with a bit of glue I could save them from the dump. So I glued them back together and they worked fine.

True to form God taught me a valuable lesson in that experience. He showed me that just because we might be broken it doesn't mean we are to be discarded. I gave that inanimate object loving, tender care and He pointed out that He would do the same for us. When I glued the headphones back together I held them until I knew they wouldn't fall apart and they were strong enough to be on their own.

But even after the glue was dry and all the pieces placed in position again I treated those headphones cautiously so that they wouldn't break again.

God does the same and more for us. May we experience His arms holding us in our broken moments and His love putting us back together again.

Prayer:
Father, I thank you that you take great care to handle us in our greatest time of need with compassion and love that surpasses any other. May we feel your arms all around us and fitting us back

together and making us whole. In Jesus name, amen.

Your thoughts:

_____
_____
_____
_____
_____
_____
_____
_____
_____
_____
_____
_____
_____
_____
_____

19. No pain, no gain

2 Corinthians 4:17
For this light momentary affliction is preparing for us an eternal weight of glory beyond comparison.

Nobody likes pain, even if we know in the end that it is all part of the process of becoming better.

Just recently I had a conversation with a friend about feet. Yes, feet. Those hard working body parts that we often take for granted. But I mentioned to her that I wanted to get a pedicure and asked for suggestions for a spa. I told her that it seemed like no matter how much lotion I applied to my feet, they always appeared dry.

She then shared some valuable advice which was shared with her. She mentioned that I needed to rub my feet almost daily with a pumice stone. If I didn't do that then there would be a build up and I would be basically putting oils and lotions on top of that and the moisture would have a hard time soaking in.

That was golden advice. I started to do an almost daily shower routine and what a difference it made. And of course the Holy Spirit pointed out the lesson. So many of us want the oil of his presence but we have such a build up of dirt that He just cannot get through.

It is time to do a daily scrub so that we are clean and God can get into our very beings. May we endure the cleaning process so that God can get the glory from our lives.

Prayer:
Father, we need you in every part of our lives. We need you to seep deep inside us. May we know that you want the best for us as we go through the process of keeping ourselves clean and scrubbing away the dirt of walking through this world. In Jesus name, amen.

Your thoughts:

20. Be careful little eyes

Proverbs 4:25-27
Look straight ahead and fix your eyes on what lies before you. Mark out a straight path for your feet, stay on the straight path. Don't get sidetracked, keep your feet on the safe path.

Ahhh! Time to relax. In typical fashion we tune out the world and tune into the tube.
One day that is exactly what I did. My mind felt like it was inundated with thought after thought and I just needed not to think. So tv it was. But almost as soon as I settled on a show I got convicted. It was full of all things ungodly, but it was really good by human, worldly standards and it was just what I needed to forget about all the concerns for an hour or two.
Or so I thought.

Holy Spirit thought differently and whispered in His usual fashion to turn the tv off. I must admit that I did reluctantly and I turned my attention to more wholesome activities.

They say the eyes are the windows to the soul and I know that whatever we watch becomes a part of us. So friend, remember the song… Oh be careful little eyes what you see? Well that's not a song just for children. May we all be careful.

Prayer:
Father may we pay attention to how we spend our time and what we let into our souls knowing that these decisions help to guide our walk. In Jesus name, amen.

Your thoughts:
_____
_____
_____
_____

21. Out of sorts

Psalm 91:1
He that dwells in the secret place of the most high shall abide under the shadow of the almighty.

The wifi was out. *Sigh*. I called the provider and reported the problem and hoped for a speedy resolution. No such luck I was told I had to wait until Friday for someone to come to fix the problem. That was four days away. What was I supposed to do without the internet for four days?

Thankfully I had data so I was still connected in some way, but there was no TV, no using the tablet. Nothing that required wifi.

I counted the days and it seemed to take forever.

When the technician came he asked all the appropriate questions and did all the checks and guess what... It was kind of my fault that the service was out. See I had recently erected a tent outside my home and the guys had damaged the cable.

Holy Spirit said, "See how you felt without wifi? How is it that you are not as bothered every time you are disconnected from me?"

I immediately felt the conviction. How about you? Are you more concerned with being able to access the internet than being able to access the creator of the universe? May we all get connected to the real source, every day all day.

Prayer:
Heavenly Father, forgive us for creating a disconnect between us and you. May we seek you first and foremost and enjoy spending time with you and love being in your secret place. In Jesus name, amen.

Your thoughts:

Made in the USA
Columbia, SC
09 January 2024